AF291444

COUNTRIES OF THE WORLD

Iran

by Shannon Anderson

BELLWETHER MEDIA • MINNEAPOLIS, MN

Blastoff! Readers are carefully developed by literacy experts to build reading stamina and move students toward fluency by combining standards-based content with developmentally appropriate text.

Level 1 provides the most support through repetition of high-frequency words, light text, predictable sentence patterns, and strong visual support.

Level 2 offers early readers a bit more challenge through varied sentences, increased text load, and text-supportive special features.

Level 3 advances early-fluent readers toward fluency through increased text load, less reliance on photos, advancing concepts, longer sentences, and more complex special features.

★ **Blastoff! Universe**

Reading Level

This edition first published in 2025 by Bellwether Media, Inc.

No part of this publication may be reproduced in whole or in part without written permission of the publisher. For information regarding permission, write to Bellwether Media, Inc., Attention: Permissions Department, 6012 Blue Circle Drive, Minnetonka, MN 55343.

Library of Congress Cataloging-in-Publication Data

LC record for Iran available at: https://lccn.loc.gov/2024012103

Editor: Suzane Nguyen   Designer: Laura Sowers

Printed in the United States of America, North Mankato, MN.

Table of Contents

Tehran

Iran is a large country in southwestern Asia. It used to be called Persia.

The country borders the Caspian Sea and two **gulfs**. Its capital is Tehran.

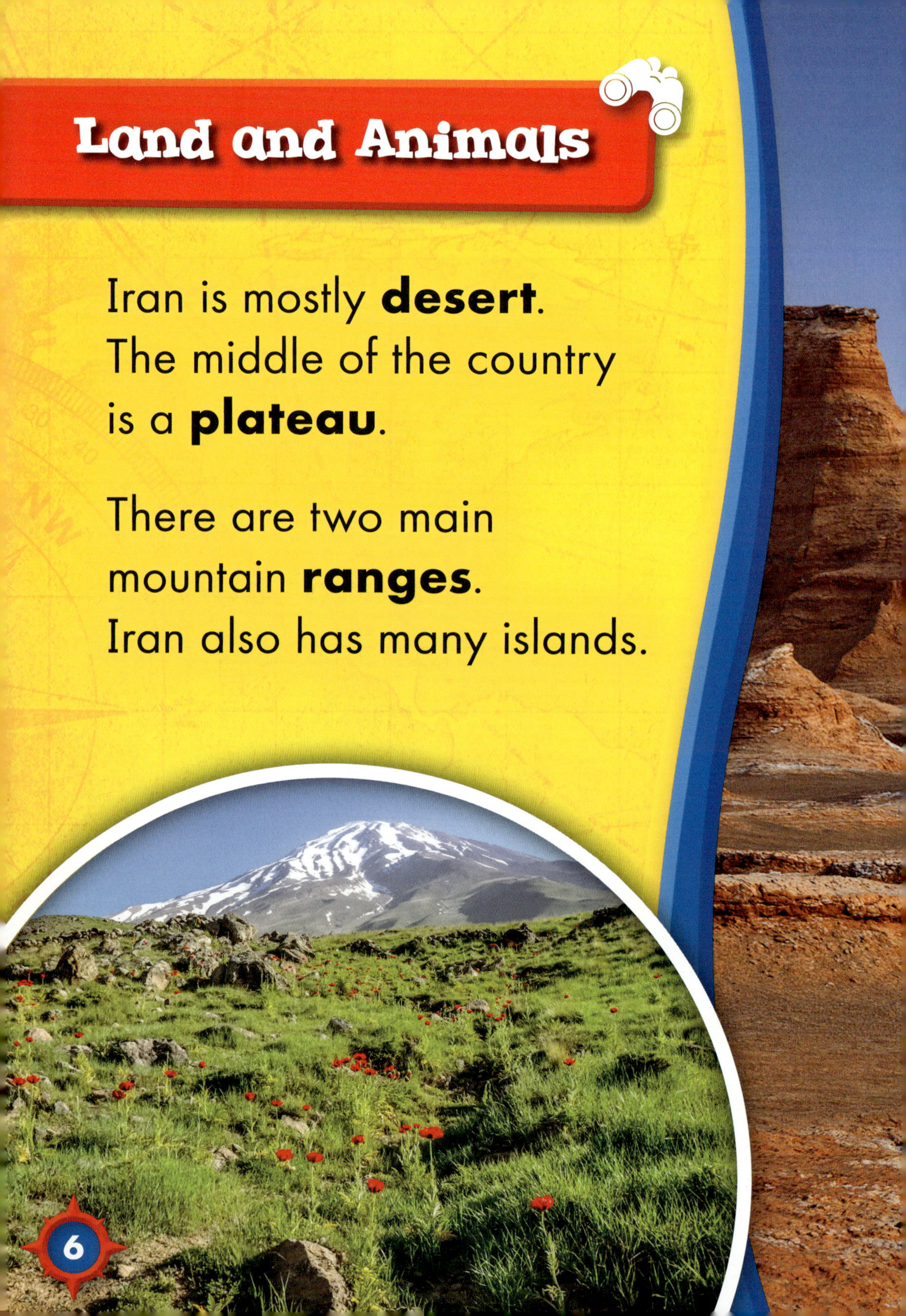

Land and Animals

Iran is mostly **desert**.
The middle of the country
is a **plateau**.

There are two main
mountain **ranges**.
Iran also has many islands.

Lut Desert
Size: 8,795 square miles
(22,780 square kilometers)
Famous For: one of the hottest
places on Earth
7

Weather in Iran depends on the land. The plateau is dry. The mountains are snowy in winter and mild in summer.

Most of the country's rain falls along the coast.

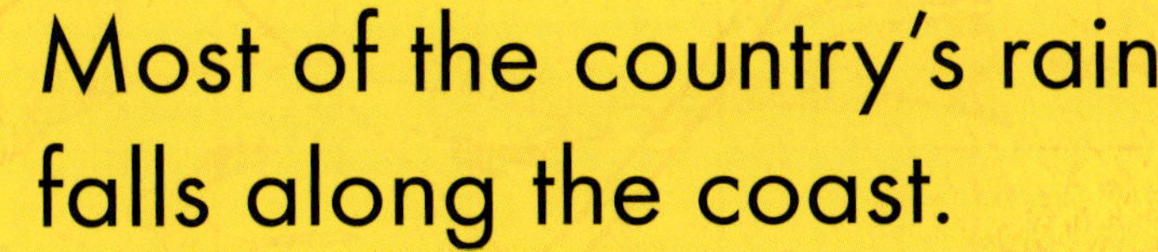

Bears roam in Iran's wooded mountains. Jackals hunt in the plateau.

cheetahs

Partridges look for seeds and leaves. The northern deserts are home to cheetahs.

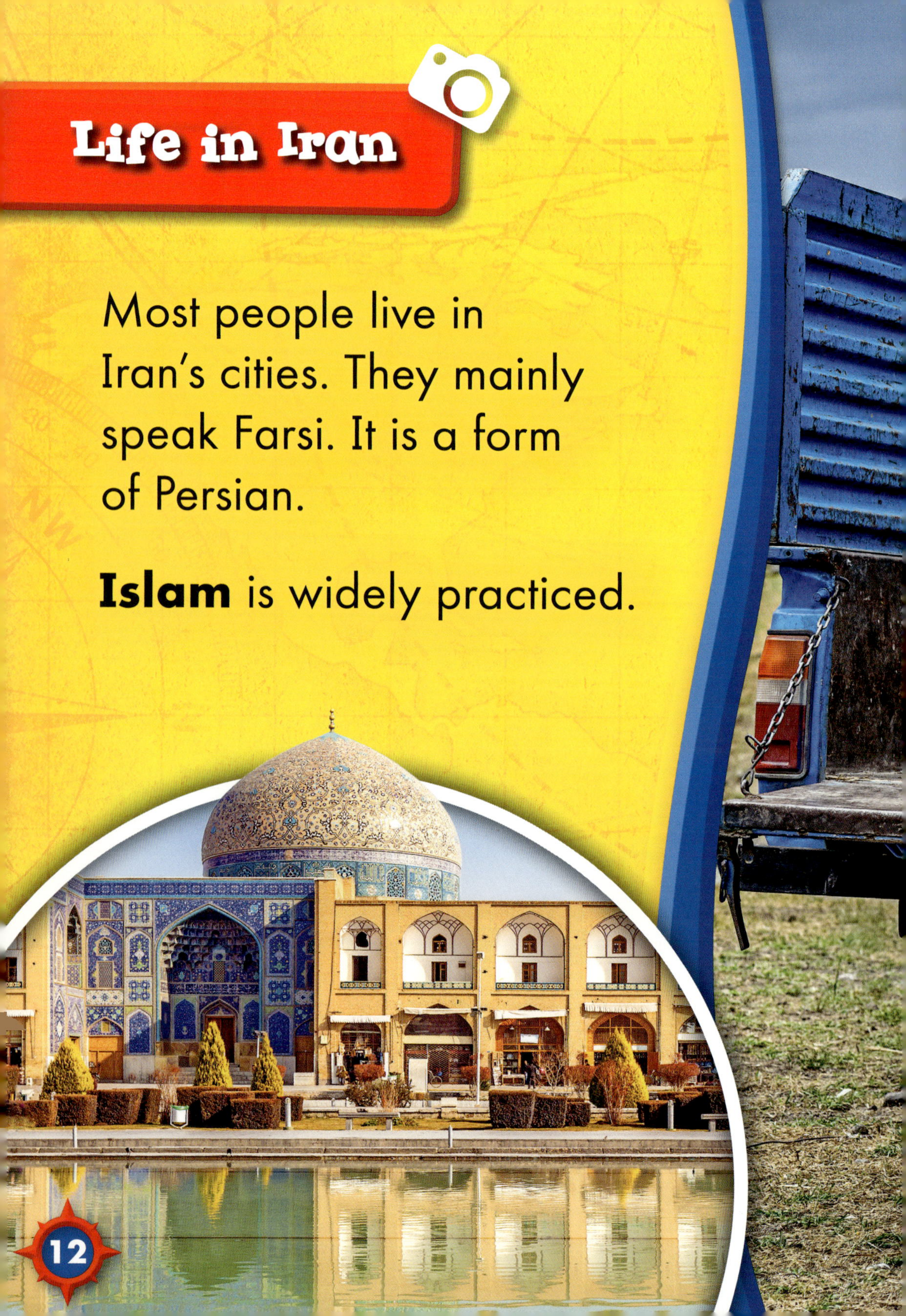

Most people live in Iran's cities. They mainly speak Farsi. It is a form of Persian.

Islam is widely practiced.

13

Iranians like to go out.
They enjoy seeing movies.

They shop for food and
handmade goods at markets.
Soccer is the most popular sport.

Lamb is a common meat dish.
Khoresh is a stew.

Iranian Foods

lamb

khoresh

kebabs

saffron

Kebabs are grilled meat on sticks.
Saffron is a popular spice.

Iranians **celebrate** *Nowruz*. It is the Iranian New Year.

Eid al-Fitr is a big day in Islam. People visit family and friends and give gifts!

Eid al-Fitr

Iran Facts

Size:
636,372 square miles
(1,648,195 square kilometers)

Population:
87,590,873 (2023)

National Holiday:
Republic Day (March 31 or April 1)

Main Language:
Persian Farsi

Capital City:
Tehran

Famous Face

Name: Narges Mohammadi
Famous For: 2023 Nobel Peace Prize winner who fights for human rights

Religions

Top Landmarks

Lake Urmia

Persepolis

Tabiat Bridge

Glossary

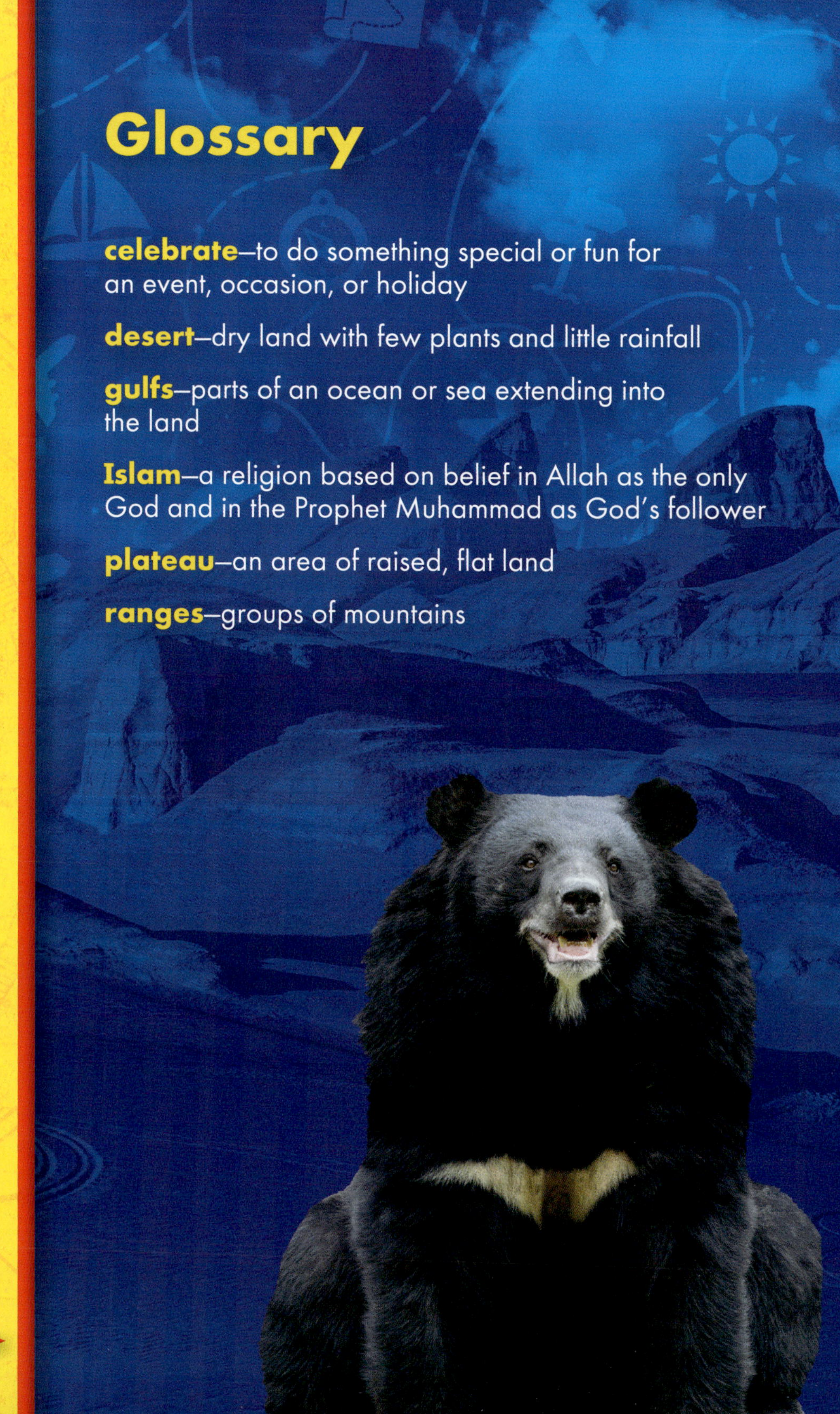

celebrate—to do something special or fun for an event, occasion, or holiday

desert—dry land with few plants and little rainfall

gulfs—parts of an ocean or sea extending into the land

Islam—a religion based on belief in Allah as the only God and in the Prophet Muhammad as God's follower

plateau—an area of raised, flat land

ranges—groups of mountains

To Learn More

AT THE LIBRARY

Ali, Marzieh A. *Ramadan and Eid al-Fitr*. Minneapolis, Minn.: Jump!, 2024.

Khorram, Adib. *Seven Special Somethings: A Nowruz Story*. New York, N.Y.: Dial Books for Young Readers, 2021.

Spanier, Kristine. *Iran*. Minneapolis, Minn.: Jump!, 2020.

ON THE WEB

FACTSURFER

Factsurfer.com gives you a safe, fun way to find more information.

1. Go to www.factsurfer.com.

2. Enter "Iran" into the search box and click 🔍.

3. Select your book cover to see a list of related content.

Index

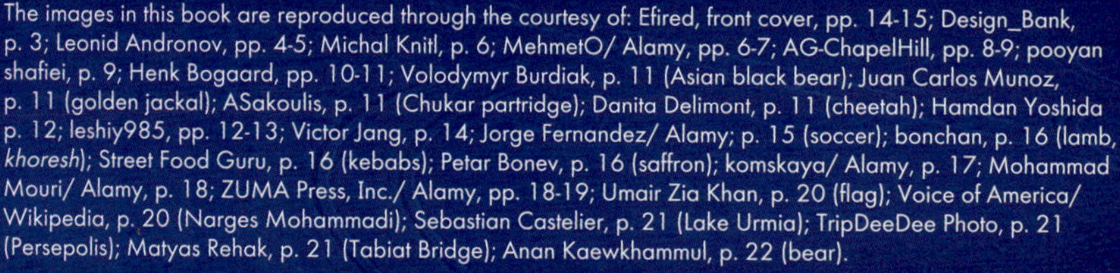

The images in this book are reproduced through the courtesy of: Efired, front cover, pp. 14-15; Design_Bank, p. 3; Leonid Andronov, pp. 4-5; Michal Knitl, p. 6; MehmetO/ Alamy, pp. 6-7; AG-ChapelHill, pp. 8-9; pooyan shafiei, p. 9; Henk Bogaard, pp. 10-11; Volodymyr Burdiak, p. 11 (Asian black bear); Juan Carlos Munoz, p. 11 (golden jackal); ASakoulis, p. 11 (Chukar partridge); Danita Delimont, p. 11 (cheetah); Hamdan Yoshida p. 12; leshiy985, pp. 12-13; Victor Jang, p. 14; Jorge Fernandez/ Alamy; p. 15 (soccer); bonchan, p. 16 (lamb, *khoresh*); Street Food Guru, p. 16 (kebabs); Petar Bonev, p. 16 (saffron); komskaya/ Alamy, p. 17; Mohammad Mouri/ Alamy, p. 18; ZUMA Press, Inc./ Alamy, pp. 18-19; Umair Zia Khan, p. 20 (flag); Voice of America/ Wikipedia, p. 20 (Narges Mohammadi); Sebastian Castelier, p. 21 (Lake Urmia); TripDeeDee Photo, p. 21 (Persepolis); Matyas Rehak, p. 21 (Tabiat Bridge); Anan Kaewkhammul, p. 22 (bear).